SEX

A D.I.Y. GUIDE

BY MARTIN BAXENDALE

© Copyright 1993 Martin Baxendale
Published by Silent but Deadly Publications,
4 Catherine's Close, Stroud, Gloucestershire

ISBN 0-9513542-9-9

Printed in Britain by Stoate & Bishop (Printers) Ltd,
Cheltenham & Gloucester. Typesetting by Alpha Studio,
The Old Convent, Beeches Green, Stroud, Glos.

CONTENTS   PAGE

AN INTRODUCTION TO THE JOY OF D.I.Y. SEX

For the keen handyman, do-it-yourself sex can prove
a relaxing and highly enjoyable pastime.

Indeed, the real joy of D.I.Y. sex is that you can
have a go virtually any time when <u>both hands</u> aren't
otherwise occupied; not just in bed but, for example,
while watching TV, lazing in the bath, reading…
MMMM!… or … AAAAH!… even … OH, YES! … while
… AAAAH!… writing … MMMM!!!… AAAHHH!!!…
OH, YES! YES! YESSSS!!!!…

Unfortunately there are many stupid superstitions and
taboos about D.I.Y. sex and the dangers of overdoing
it. Ignore them all. Do-it-yourself sex is perfectly
natural, normal and safe — no more dangerous than
crossing the road or driving to work (Note: we do
not, however, recommend practising D.I.Y. sex <u>while</u>
crossing the road or driving to work).

So don't worry, it's nothing to be ashamed of or
feel guilty about in any way at all. Just about
everyone does it or has done it at some time or
another (except the author, of course . . . not ME!
Never needed to. NO WAY! You wouldn't catch
<u>ME</u> doing it, mate!)

Editor's note: Not unless you know his secret
hiding places!

DISCLAIMER: Please note that the author and publisher accept <u>no liability</u> for any personal injury, marital problems, social embarrassment, criminal prosecution or any other consequences whatsoever arising as a result of advice given in this manual.

In particular, we accept no liability or blame in the event of anyone going blind, going incurably mad, getting hairy palms, or burning in Hell for all eternity.

The author would also like to point out that the advice given in this handbook is purely theoretical and is in <u>no way whatsoever</u> based on any practical experience or personal experimentation by the author himself (either with or without the aid of any mechanical devices or small domestic pets). Furthermore, that the incident involving the cantaloupe melon and the hand of bananas in the fruit and veg. aisle of Tescos widely reported in the national Press was an unfortunate misunderstanding, and that all charges against the author have now been dropped following a police caution.

NOTE: For the convenience of readers, the cover of this manual has been treated with a specially – developed rubberised extra-grip surface material, ensuring a firm hold and making it easier to consult while you have a D.I.Y. sex job in hand.

GETTING STARTED

If you're a beginner, turning your hand to D.I.Y. sex for the first time, getting started is fairly simple and straightforward. Anyone who is reasonably good with his hands should find that it comes easy after a little practice.

ESSENTIAL TOOLS: Unlike many other, more expensive, D.I.Y. hobbies, do-it-yourself sex does not generally require a large tool kit. You should find that you can manage perfectly well with whatever odd tool you happen to have hanging around.

A large tool box is also, therefore, not necessary (unless of course you have an exceptionally huge tool or just like to boast).

NOTE: It is considered, in do-it-yourself sex circles as much as in other forms of D.I.Y., extremely bad manners to use someone else's tool without their express permission, and may lead to long-running arguments with neighbours, a severe duffing-up, or criminal charges.

CHOOSING A PARTNER: Compatability with your partner is vital. Try to choose a partner that you get on easily with and, if in doubt, go for what feels <u>right</u> (or <u>left</u> as the case may be).

Special note for <u>ambidextrous</u> do-it-yourselfers: LUCKY F***ING BASTARDS!!!

SEX BEFORE MARRIAGE: D.I.Y. sex is frequently practised before, during and after marriage. This is quite normal.

You should also find that, in these more enlightened times, there is little social pressure to marry your D.I.Y. sex partner (unless of course you're unfortunate enough to belong to an extremely strict and orthodox religious sect, or have very wierd family and friends).

However, any private and personal little unofficial ceremony you might feel moved to devise, in order to demonstrate your commitment to your partner, is up to you.

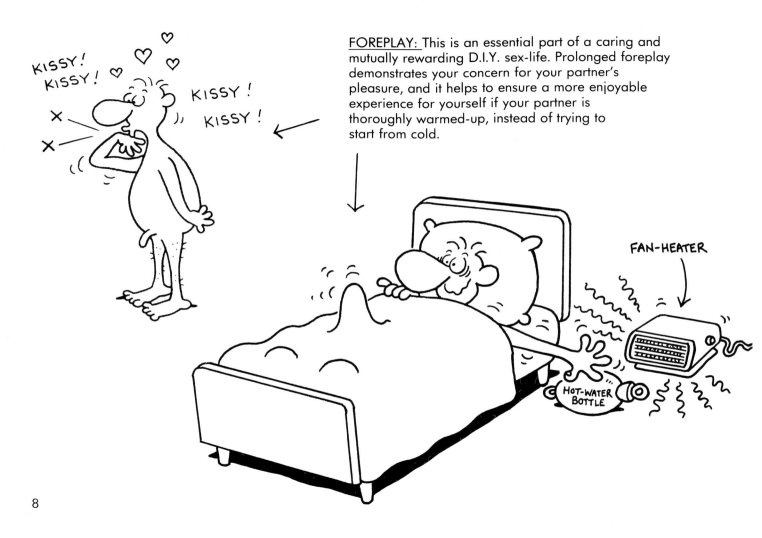

FOREPLAY: This is an essential part of a caring and mutually rewarding D.I.Y. sex-life. Prolonged foreplay demonstrates your concern for your partner's pleasure, and it helps to ensure a more enjoyable experience for yourself if your partner is thoroughly warmed-up, instead of trying to start from cold.

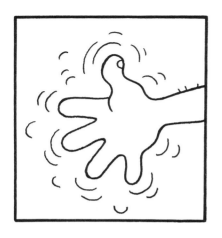

HEALTH RISKS, HAZARDS, PROBLEMS AND PRECAUTIONS

PHYSICAL INJURY: Most serious potential risk is the danger of developing repetitive stress injury (similar to that commonly experienced by computer keyboard operators) caused by prolonged repetitive hand movements. If indulging in frequent and sustained D.I.Y. sex activities over extended periods, we strongly recommend that you take regular breaks and change hands occasionally. In the event of serious injury, refer immediately to doctor. See also section on 'D.I.Y. Sex Without The Effort' later in this book.

Common minor injuries such as blisters and friction burns are a less serious problem, although they can be annoying, and generally require medical attention or hospitalization only in the most severe cases.

If these do occur, slow down and/or use a recommended lubricant (see below). Protective rubber gloves and/or condoms (both suitably lubricated) will provide added protection but can reduce sensitivity. Suitable extra-thin disposable gloves are available from the washing-up gloves displays of many supermarkets. Don't be embarrassed to buy them; it's better than getting blisters! (See also section on 'D.I.Y. Sex Aids').

The alternative is to 'toughen' the affected areas, building up blister-resistant calloused skin and

9

tissue by repeated plunging into a sand-box (as practised by some karate experts) or repeated pickling. However, this is not recommended too strongly (especially as an anti-blister precaution for willies) except for D.I.Y. sado-masochists (see later section on this for further hints).

RECOMMENDED LUBRICANTS: These include: Vaseline, KY jelly, hand-cream, moisturising lotion, baby oil, olive oil, grape-seed oil, walnut oil, peanut butter, custard, yoghurt, fromage frais, 'deep heat' rub ointment (for D.I.Y. sado-masochists), sun-tan lotion (for outdoor freaks) etc, according to taste and what's close to hand when you feel the urge.

GOING BLIND AND/OR MAD: Highly unlikely; just stupid superstitions and old wives' tales. Take no notice of them. (Note: This manual is also widely available in an inexpensive Braille edition).

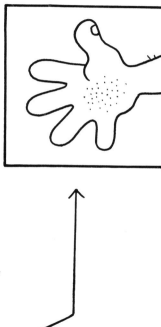

HAIRY PALMS: Another ridiculous superstition, as any intelligent person knows. However, just to be on the safe side, a regular hair-removing wax treatment is an excellent preventative measure. Electrolysis or mechanical hair removal would probably do just as well. Warning: regular shaving of palms can result in unsightly and painful stubble.

EMBARRASSING DISCOVERY: Always a risk; but getting caught in the act shouldn't be a problem for any well-adjusted sex do-it-yourselfer. After all, it's perfectly normal and natural. But oh my God! Think of the EMBARRASSMENT!!! The SHAME!!! The GUILT!!!

Should the unthinkable actually happen, we suggest the following immediate course of emergency action:
1) Promise never, ever to do it again.
2) Say your prayers every night for a week.
3) Find a sympathetic and inexpensive therapist.
4) Find some new hiding places.

Better still, make sure that at all times you have some convincing excuses prepared, such as:
a) You were just relieving an excruciating bout of cramp in your willy.
b) Poor blood circulation problems require that, on medical advice, you regularly and vigorously massage all extremities (but don't push your luck and ask for help with this).
c) In the dark, you mistook your willy for someone else's.
d) You've got a flat tyre on your bicycle and you mistook your willy for the bicycle pump. Should an observant person ask where the bicycle is, look surprised and say 'Shit! Some bastard's nicked it!' (Note: This excuse is not guaranteed to work in your bedroom in the middle of the night, but if you can't think of anything else, it's worth a try).

UNWANTED PREGNANCY: Nothing to worry about here. Your D.I.Y. sex partner is extremely unlikely to become pregnant, so there is no need to take precautions against this (although use of lubricated condoms and washing-up gloves <u>can</u> help to relieve chronic blister or friction-burn problems; see above).

Should your partner swell up, this is probably due simply to over-doing things (see 'Repetitive Stress Injury'). Try taking a break.

11

BOOSTING YOUR D.I.Y. SEX LIFE AND AVOID BOREDOM

It's all too easy for any D.I.Y. sex life to lose its thrill and become boring if you and your do-it-yourself partner allow yourselves to slip into a dull routine with no variety or inventiveness.

It's especially important in a loving and caring D.I.Y. relationship to watch out for those tell-tale little signs of boredom from your partner, which suggest that things aren't quite as wonderful and exciting as they used to be.

Keep an eye out during D.I.Y. sex for typical giveaway signals from your partner like: Fingers tapping, twiddling, drumming or picking your nose in a bored and absent-minded manner, when they should be concentrating on the job in hand. Note: It's a dead giveaway that the magic has gone when your partner <u>goes to sleep</u> in the middle of sex.

Don't take this as a hurtful or intentional rejection, but simply as a sign that your D.I.Y. sex life is in need of a boost.

"WAS IT GOOD FOR YOU TOO?"

Don't, however, get too obsessive about always looking for signs that your partner is enjoying it as much as you, otherwise things can become very tense and you'll simply make matters worse.

In particular, do not expect your partner to always have earth-shattering multiple orgasms. It's a well-known fact that D.I.Y. sex partners can't reach orgasm so quickly and easily as you can. Prolonged foreplay (see 'Getting Started') may help (or not).

You'll often find that a sensitive and considerate partner will sometimes <u>fake</u> it, to add to your enjoyment and boost your ego (although this may turn out to be just a symptom of overdoing things, repetitive stress injury, or a heavy session in the boozer the night before).

<u>SEXUAL TECHNIQUE TIP:</u> You may find that a swift tap on the funny-bone with a small hammer will help to induce swift orgasm in your partner if it's taking too long.

D.I.Y. sex is most satisfying and mutually enjoyable if you and your partner both finish <u>together.</u> Mutual simultaneous orgasm can often be ensured by employing the above technique with your spare hand at just the right moment.

The following sections of this manual provide further and more detailed advice and useful hints on keeping your D.I.Y. sex life fresh and exciting.

D.I.Y. SEX POSITIONS

Variety is the essence of an exciting and fulfilling do-it-yourself sex life, so be adventurous in your choice of positions rather than sticking to the same boring old one every time. Here are some of the more basic positions you can experiment with:

'STANDING'

'LYING DOWN'

'SITTING DOWN'

'BENDING-OVER, FROM BEHIND'

D.I.Y. SEX SITUATIONS

Where you do it can be just as important as how you do it when it comes to adding variety and spice to your D.I.Y. sex life and preventing boredom setting in. Here are a few suggestions for alternatives to the boring old bedroom-with-the-lights-off setting.

IN THE BATH
An ideal relaxing situation to try your hand at some leisurely D.I.Y.

Warnings: Don't let the water get cold or you could experience 'droop' problems. Also resist any temptation to experiment with plugholes or taps as D.I.Y. sex aids; this can lead to considerable embarrassment and cost if you have to call out an emergency plumber or the fire brigade to get you free.

WASHING MITT (with stimulating towelling texture)

SOME USEFUL BATHTIME D.I.Y. ACCESSORIES:

LUXURY HAND SOAP D.I.Y. SEX AID

HAND SOAP

STIMULATING AND INVIGORATING D.I.Y. SEX AID SHOWER FITTING

WATCHING TV

A situation in which boring moments (commercial breaks, party political broadcasts, Queen's Xmas speech, etc) can be enlivened with a quick spot of do-it-yourself.

Warning: Not recommended while eating hot TV dinners (unless you're into D.I.Y. sado-masochism and relish the danger of hot-gravy scalds).

Note: If embarrassingly caught in the act while watching television, a good standby excuse is to claim that you absent-mindedly mistook your willy for the TV remote control.

DOING THE HOUSEWORK

A bit of impromptu D.I.Y. will equally help to make doing dull household chores less tiresome. However, the potential for accidents is considerable, especially around domestic appliances, so take care.

The rythmic vibrations from various electrical domestic appliances can prove quite stimulating, as many a housewife can tell you. However, the male do-it-yourselfer needs to be particularly cautious to avoid dangers of becoming inadvertently trapped, entangled and mangled in moving parts. Be especially wary of things like food-processors, liquidisers, juice extractors and coffee grinders (see also section on 'Vibrators' under 'Sex Aids').

Take special care in the kitchen, where serious domestic accidents like hot-fat burns, scalds and electrocution in wet situations are all too common.

We particularly recommend the greatest caution if indulging in a little D.I.Y. sex while frying <u>sausages</u> as this situation can lead to some very unfortunate mix-ups and accidents. There is also a general danger in any cooking situation that an engrossed do-it-yourselfer may absent-mindly use whatever happens to be in his hand to stir a boiling pot or scrape out the bottom of the food processor.

D.I.Y. sex while hoovering carries serious risks and calls for caution. Do remember that the suction from vacuum cleaners can be very strong and potentially painful if carelessly pointed in the wrong direction. <u>Don't be tempted to experiment!</u>

Do-it-yourself sex while ironing can also prove hazardous and demands alertness at all times, to ensure that you don't end up ironing a <u>pink tie</u> that you didn't know you had.

VROOOM!

SUCK!

OUT OF DOORS

This situation always makes for a refreshing change. But if you and your D.I.Y. sex partner are open-spaces freaks, it's safest to confine yourselves to the privacy of a well-hedged garden not overlooked by neighbouring houses or office blocks, if you're to avoid a court appearance (note: Courtrooms are <u>not</u> recommended situations for D.I.Y. sex . . . unless you're stuck on jury service at a particularly long and tedious trial).

SUNBATHING

An ideal relaxing situation for a bit of leisurely do-it-yourself, provided your garden offers adequate privacy (see previous comments).

Warning: We very strongly recommend the use of suntan oil as a lubricant in this situation, to help avoid the very real danger of painful and embarrassing sunburn.

GARDENING

Given assured privacy, do-it-yourself sex is easily combined with a spot of gardening without too much danger of embarrassing discovery. But do try not to disturb the wildlife, as being interrupted by visitors while apparently flashing (or worse) at a passing hedgehog coud conceivably result in a prosecution by the R.S.P.C.A.

Gardening gloves are widely available in a range of stimulating materials, from excitingly ribbed rubber to rough-textured leather (for those who like that sort of thing). A padded kneeling stool is always a useful purchase to ensure added comfort, especially for the more elderly (and just as useful for weeding).

The risk of being caught in the act if interrupted in the garden can be considerably reduced by wearing at all times a <u>green condom</u> liberally sprinkled with greenfly, and keeping a spray-can handy.

In addition to acting as excellent camouflage in the flower border, this simple ruse lends itself to useful cover-up lines like "I'm just pulling a few weeds" or "Just spraying the greenfly" (also possible as an excuse without the green condom if caught just at the critical moment, but even less likely to be believed).

Useful as the above suggestion can prove in most gardening situations, we do <u>not</u> recommend its use during pruning operations, when the potential for horrendous mistakes is all too obvious.

THE ELEMENT OF SURPRISE

Another handy device to help liven up a flagging D.I.Y. sex life is to introduce the element of surprise into your boring old routines, constantly trying to catch your partner unawares with potential do-it-yourself situations at unexpected moments.

For a start, try cutting the bottoms out of your trouser pockets, so that your D.I.Y. sex partner will unintentionally encounter your willy when searching for small change, matches, etc. or simply when trying to warm up in cold weather. Always a pleasant surprise, and one which can lead to many an unplanned and exciting bit of D.I.Y.

Here are a few suggestions for some other tricks you can try along similar lines:

Stand by 'phone and replace telephone handset with willy, so that when it rings and your D.I.Y. partner reaches to answer . . . surprise, surprise!

Before doing washing-up, disguise willy as 'squeezy' washing-up liquid bottle . . . and see how much more one little squeeze will do! An added bonus here is that your D.I.Y. sex partner may well be alluringly and excitingly dressed in a sexy rubber washing-up glove (see also 'D.I.Y. Sex Aids').

In car, disguise willy by balancing gear-knob on end. Start-up, clutch in . . . and off you go! Warning: We recommend that you attempt this only while stationary (and preferably in the privacy of your own garage). If not a car owner, try letting the air out of your bicycle tyres and clipping willy to the cross-bar in place of bicycle pump, for a similar unexpected encounter with your D.I.Y. sex partner.

D.I.Y. SEX FANTASIES

Fantasising during D.I.Y. sex with your chosen partner is perfectly natural, a common occurence and nothing to feel guilty about even if your fantasies are about <u>another</u> D.I.Y. sex partner.

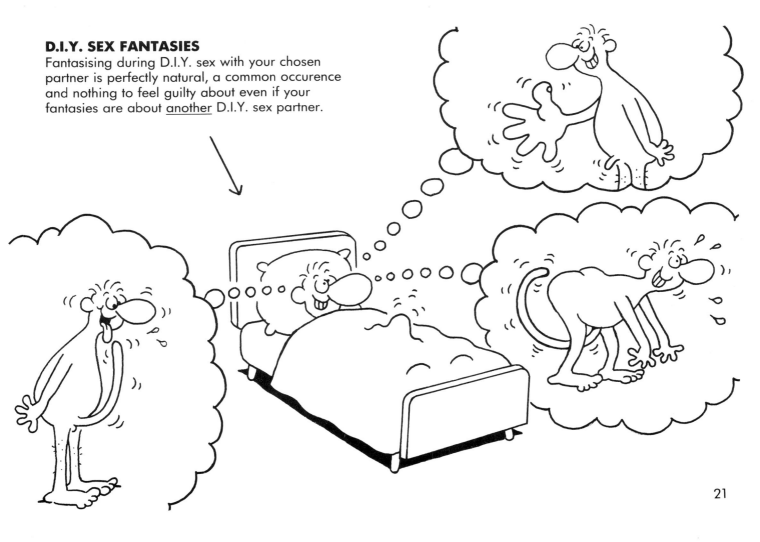

SWOPPING PARTNERS

This too can add interest to your D.I.Y. sex life and is common practice amongst do-it-yourselfers. It also helps to reduce the risk of developing repetitive stress injury (see 'Health Risks, Hazards, Problems and Precautions).

Swopping partners can also lead to yet another fun D.I.Y. sex variation – three in a bed. While this can add excitement to your do-it-yourself sex life, it unfortunately means that you won't be able to read a bedtime book or drink your cocoa at the same time, but then you can't have everything.

Note: Swopping D.I.Y. sex partners with someone else doesn't count as do-it-yourself, especially if you bring in a professional to lend a hand with a D.I.Y. job (this is widely considered to be cheating).

BONDAGE

This can be fun as well, provided it's with the full consent of all parties involved and doesn't lead to any real injury or serious discomfort.

Note: We do not recommend the usual sexual technique of tying <u>both hands</u> to the bed posts. This can lead to serious difficulties (as you will very soon discover).

ONE HAND TIED
BEHIND BACK

D.I.Y. SADO-MASOCHISM

Sandy beaches are a very good choice of situation for D.I.Y. sex if you're into sado-masochism; amongst the dunes on the sort of hot, dry windy day that will guarantee gritty sand getting into every tender and sensitive nook and cranny of your most private anatomy (with the possible added bonus of extremely intimate and painful sunburn).

Better still, in the middle of a desert sand-storm is the D.I.Y. sado-masochist's ultimate fantasy, but unfortunately only available to those who can afford expensive North African sun-and-sand holidays.

An acceptable substitute for these outdoor situations can be created at home with a bag of builder's sand and a sun lamp, although a sand-pit in the corner of your bedroom may prove difficult to explain away if discovered (unless you have a lot of very large cats around the house).

For beginners, we would recommend starting a little less painfully; say with a spot of D.I.Y. sex after breakfast in bed, when the sheets should be suitably full of gritty and irritating toast crumbs.

Note: Long fingernails are an essential aid to D.I.Y. sado-masochism. Most practitioners also find Deep Heat rub an ideal D.I.Y. sex lubricant; but do avoid using sun-tan lotion outdoors, to help ensure the added extra of painful genital sunburn. See also 'D.I.Y. Sex Aids'.

D.I.Y. SEX AIDS

VIBRATORS

Various household appliances can double-up as handy D.I.Y. sex vibrators. However, take great care at all times, as experimentation with some of the more dangerous appliances to be found in the home and garden can prove extremely hazardous if not handled with caution (see also 'D.I.Y. Sex Situations').

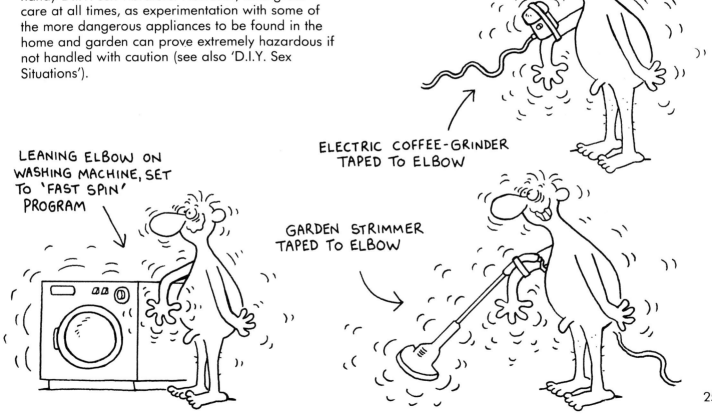

ELECTRIC COFFEE-GRINDER TAPED TO ELBOW

LEANING ELBOW ON WASHING MACHINE, SET TO 'FAST SPIN' PROGRAM

GARDEN STRIMMER TAPED TO ELBOW

25

D.I.Y. SEX AIDS (continued)

<u>DRESSING-UP YOUR D.I.Y. SEX PARTNER:</u>
Getting your partner to dress-up sexily for you can give your D.I.Y. sex life a real boost, and these days most supermarket chains are broad-minded enough to openly stock a wide range of the do-it-yourself sex expert's most basic accessory — the rubber washing-up glove.

These are now commonly available off the supermarket shelf in a wide range of exciting and useful styles. According to taste, look out for the following types on your next trip to Tesco's or Sainsbury's:

'LIGHTWEIGHT' (for ultra-sensitivity); 'HEAVY DUTY' (for extended and extra-heavy use); 'RIBBED EXTRA-GRIP' (for added stimulation, and a firm hold in slippery conditions); extra thin see-through 'DISPOSABLE' (for that exciting peek-a-boo look, and for lovers-lane-style 'use and throw away' quickies).

STUDDED LEATHER BIKERS GLOVE
(for leather freaks)

CHAIN-MAIL GAUNTLET (for D.I.Y. sado-masochists;
widely available from fancy dress hire shops).

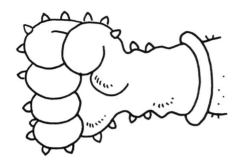

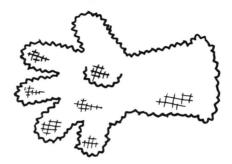

'SEXY SUSIE' HAND-PUPPET

'PUNCH-AND-JUDY' HAND-PUPPET
(for D.I.Y. sexual domination freaks).

'HANDY MANDY' INFLATABLE D.I.Y. SEX DOLL

RUBBER TONGUE EXTENSION

D.I.Y. SEX AIDS (continued)

With the aid of an inexpensive video camera, it's now quite a simple matter to make and view your own D.I.Y. sex films at home, adding yet another exciting dimension to your do-it-yourself sex-life.

Warning: Keep D.I.Y. sex videos out of the reach of children, and try to resist the temptation to bore visitors with them (although they may just conceivably be of some interest to any visiting palm-readers).

D.I.Y. SEX WITHOUT THE EFFORT

These suggestions for reduced-effort D.I.Y. sex
may prove particularly useful to older do-it-
yourselfers, but are equally valuable for everyday
use to help reduce the risk of developing repetitive
stress injury due to prolonged regular D.I.Y.
activities (see also 'Health Risks, Hazards,
Problems and Precautions').

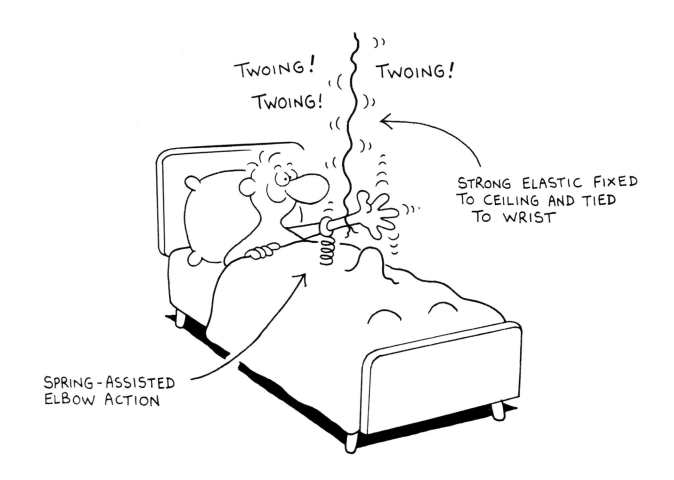